ALEX STIRLING

The Prompt Engineer's Handbook

Unlocking Wealth through Words and Images

Contents

1 The Art and Science of Prompt Engineering   1

2 Introduction to Prompt Engineering   4

3 AI and Large Language Models (LLMs)   8

4 Crafting the Perfect AI Prompt   12

5 Applied AI Prompting   16

6 Text and Image Models   21

7 Emerging Models in AI   26

8 Developing a Prompt Engineering Mindset   31

9 Best Practices in Prompt Engineering   36

10 Zero-Shot and Few-Shot Prompting   40

11 Chain of Thought Prompting   44

12 AI Hallucinations and Error Handling   48

13 Vectors and Text Embeddings in AI   52

14 Maintaining and Updating Prompt Libraries   56

15 Reporting and Analytics in Prompt Engineering   60

16 Case Studies and Real-World Applications   64

17 The Future of Prompt Engineering   69

1

The Art and Science of Prompt Engineering

Welcome to "The Prompt Engineer's Handbook: Unlocking Wealth through Words and Images"

In the dynamic intersection of language, technology, and creativity, prompt engineering emerges as a pivotal skill in the era of advanced artificial intelligence (AI). This handbook is designed to be an essential guide for anyone looking to master the art of communicating with AI, harnessing its capabilities to generate wealth through words and images.

The Essence of Prompt Engineering

At its core, prompt engineering is about crafting effective prompts - inputs that guide AI models, particularly in natural language processing (NLP) and image generation, to produce desired outputs. It's a skill that blends linguistic acuity, technical understanding, and creative insight, enabling us to unlock the full potential of AI tools like ChatGPT, DALL-E, and others.

Why Prompt Engineering?

In a world increasingly reliant on AI for content creation, data analysis, customer interaction, and more, the ability to effectively communicate with AI systems is crucial. Well-designed prompts can lead to insightful, accurate, and contextually appropriate responses, opening up a wealth of opportunities in various domains.

Navigating the Handbook

This handbook is structured to take you on a comprehensive journey through the world of prompt engineering:

1. **Foundational Concepts**: We begin by laying the groundwork, introducing you to the basics of AI and the principles of prompt engineering.
2. **Advanced Techniques**: As we progress, the book delves into more sophisticated strategies like zero-shot learning, chain of thought prompting, and handling AI hallucinations.
3. **Practical Applications**: Through a series of case studies, we explore real-world applications, demonstrating how prompt engineering is applied in different industries.
4. **Future Trends**: Finally, we look ahead, discussing emerging trends and preparing you for the future advancements in AI and prompt engineering.

For Whom Is This Book?

Whether you're a seasoned AI enthusiast, a content creator, a business professional, or someone curious about the potential of AI, this book offers valuable insights and practical knowledge. It's for anyone who seeks to leverage the power of AI in crafting compelling narratives, generating innovative ideas, or improving business processes through intelligent automation.

Embarking on a Journey of Discovery

As you turn these pages, you'll embark on a journey of discovery. You'll learn not just how to communicate with AI, but how to think alongside it, unlocking creative and professional possibilities that were once the realm of science fiction.

Welcome to "The Prompt Engineer's Handbook." Let's begin this exciting journey together, exploring the limitless potential of AI through the lens of prompt engineering.

2

Introduction to Prompt Engineering

Understanding the Basics of Prompt Engineering

In the rapidly evolving world of artificial intelligence (AI), prompt engineering emerges as a crucial discipline, bridging the gap between human intention and AI comprehension. This chapter introduces the foundational concepts of prompt engineering, its significance, and its role in enhancing interactions with large language models (LLMs) like ChatGPT.

The Genesis of Prompt Engineering

Prompt engineering is born out of the necessity to communicate effectively with AI systems. As AI technologies, particularly in natural language processing, have advanced, the need for structured, clear, and purposeful prompts has become paramount. This discipline involves crafting, refining, and optimizing prompts – the inputs given to AI systems – to elicit the most accurate and relevant responses.

Why Prompt Engineering?

The essence of prompt engineering lies in its ability to transform vague or ambiguous human queries into structured requests that AI can understand and process efficiently. This is crucial because AI, despite its advanced algorithms, still relies on the quality of input to generate quality output. Poorly structured prompts can lead to irrelevant, incorrect, or confusing responses, whereas well-engineered prompts can unlock the full potential of AI, leading to insightful, accurate, and contextually appropriate responses.

The Role of Prompt Engineering in AI Interactions

Prompt engineering is not just about the technical aspect of writing prompts. It's an art that combines understanding of linguistics, psychology, and the specific mechanics of AI models. A prompt engineer must consider various factors: the model's capabilities, the context of the query, the desired outcome, and potential biases or limitations of the AI.

The Evolution of AI and Its Impact on Prompt Engineering

To appreciate the role of prompt engineering, one must understand the evolution of AI. Early AI systems were rule-based, relying on strict programming and specific commands. However, with the advent of machine learning and, more recently, deep learning, AI systems have become more sophisticated, capable of understanding and generating human-like text.

LLMs like ChatGPT represent the pinnacle of this evolution. They are trained on vast datasets and can generate coherent and contextually relevant text based on the prompts they receive. However, their performance is heavily dependent on how these prompts are structured.

The Science Behind Prompt Engineering

At its core, prompt engineering is about understanding how LLMs interpret and process language. These models use complex algorithms to analyze text, identify patterns, and generate responses. The effectiveness of these responses hinges on the clarity and specificity of the prompts.

Crafting Effective Prompts

Effective prompt engineering involves several key elements:

1. **Clarity**: The prompt must be clear and unambiguous. AI models can misinterpret vague or poorly structured prompts, leading to unsatisfactory responses.
2. **Context**: Providing context helps the AI understand the prompt's background, leading to more accurate and relevant responses.
3. **Conciseness**: While detail is important, overly verbose prompts can confuse AI models. Striking a balance between brevity and completeness is essential.
4. **Creativity**: Sometimes, eliciting the best response from an AI requires creative phrasing or structuring of prompts.

Challenges in Prompt Engineering

Despite its potential, prompt engineering is not without challenges. One of the primary challenges is dealing with the inherent limitations and biases of AI models. AI systems are only as good as the data they are trained on, and they can inherit biases present in their training datasets. Prompt engineers must be aware of these limitations and craft prompts that mitigate these biases.

The Future of Prompt Engineering

As AI continues to advance, the role of prompt engineering will become even more significant. We are moving towards a future where AI will be an integral part of many aspects of life, from business and education to healthcare and entertainment. The ability to effectively communicate with AI systems will be a critical skill, and prompt engineering will be at the forefront of this interaction.

Conclusion

Prompt engineering is a fascinating and rapidly growing field that sits at the intersection of technology, language, and human psychology. It plays a crucial role in maximizing the effectiveness of AI systems, particularly in natural language processing. As we continue to advance in our journey with AI, the skills and techniques of prompt engineering will become increasingly vital in unlocking the full potential of these extraordinary technologies.

3

AI and Large Language Models (LLMs)

The Landscape of Artificial Intelligence

To delve into the realm of prompt engineering, it's essential to understand the broader landscape of artificial intelligence (AI) and its evolution. AI, at its core, is the simulation of human intelligence processes by machines, especially computer systems. These processes include learning, reasoning, problem-solving, perception, and language understanding.

The Evolution of AI

The journey of AI has been a fascinating one, starting from simple rule-based systems to the complex neural networks we see today. Early AI was limited to executing predefined tasks and lacked the ability to learn or adapt. The advent of machine learning changed this, enabling systems to learn from data and improve over time. The real game-changer, however, has been the development of deep learning, a subset of machine learning based on artificial neural networks. This has led to unprecedented advancements in AI capabilities, particularly in processing and generating human language.

Understanding Large Language Models (LLMs)

At the heart of modern AI's language capabilities are Large Language Models (LLMs) like ChatGPT. LLMs are a type of deep learning model designed to understand, interpret, and generate human language. They are 'large' both in terms of the size of the neural networks (often consisting of billions of parameters) and the vast amount of data they are trained on.

How LLMs Work

LLMs work by processing text input and predicting the next word in a sequence, learning patterns and structures in language through their training data. This allows them to generate text that is coherent, contextually relevant, and often indistinguishable from human-written text. The training process involves exposing the model to a large corpus of text, enabling it to learn a wide range of language styles, tones, and content.

The Significance of LLMs in Prompt Engineering

The advent of LLMs has revolutionized the field of prompt engineering. The ability of these models to understand and generate complex text has opened up new possibilities for human-AI interaction. However, the effectiveness of these interactions largely depends on the quality of the prompts given to the AI. This is where prompt engineering plays a pivotal role.

Best Practices in Interacting with LLMs

Interacting with LLMs requires an understanding of their strengths and limitations. Here are some key considerations:

1. **Contextual Understanding**: LLMs are adept at understanding context, but the clarity of the prompt is crucial. Providing sufficient context ensures more accurate and relevant responses.
2. **Handling Ambiguity**: LLMs can struggle with ambiguity. Clear and specific prompts help in eliciting the desired response.
3. **Creativity and Flexibility**: LLMs can generate creative and varied content, but they need direction. Creative prompting can lead to more innovative and useful outputs.

Challenges in Working with LLMs

While LLMs are powerful, they are not without challenges:

1. **Data Bias**: LLMs can reflect biases present in their training data. Prompt engineers must be aware of these biases and work to mitigate them.
2. **Understanding Limitations**: LLMs may not always understand or generate accurate technical, factual, or nuanced content. Recognizing these limitations is key to effective prompt engineering.
3. **Ethical Considerations**: The use of LLMs raises ethical questions, particularly around privacy, misinformation, and the potential for misuse. Prompt engineers must navigate these issues carefully.

Applications of LLMs

LLMs have a wide range of applications, from content creation and customer service to language translation and educational tools. Each application requires a unique approach to prompt engineering, tailored to the specific needs and goals of the task.

The Future of LLMs

The field of LLMs is rapidly evolving, with ongoing research and development. Future models are likely to be more accurate, context-aware, and capable of handling more complex tasks. This will further enhance the role of prompt engineering in shaping effective human-AI interactions.

Conclusion

Large Language Models represent a significant leap forward in AI's ability to process and generate human language. They are the engines driving the new era of AI-powered communication and creativity. However, harnessing their full potential requires skillful prompt engineering, balancing technical know-how with an understanding of language, psychology, and ethics. As we move forward, the synergy between LLMs and prompt engineering will continue to be a key factor in the advancement of AI and its integration into our daily lives.

4

Crafting the Perfect AI Prompt

In the realm of artificial intelligence, particularly with models like GPT-4, the quality of the output is heavily influenced by the quality of the input. This chapter delves into the intricacies of crafting the perfect prompt, ensuring that you can harness the full potential of AI models for various applications.

Understanding the Basics

Before diving into the specifics of prompt crafting, it's essential to understand what a prompt is. A prompt is the initial input given to an AI model to generate a response. It can be a question, a statement, or a set of instructions. The goal is to provide clear and concise information that guides the AI to produce the desired output.

Key Elements of a Good Prompt

1. Clarity: The prompt should be clear and unambiguous. Avoid using vague terms or complex language that might confuse the AI.
2. Specificity: Be specific about what you want. The more detailed

your prompt, the better the AI can understand and respond.

3. Context: Provide enough context to help the AI understand the background and nuances of the request.

4. Conciseness: While being specific, also strive to be concise. Long-winded prompts can lead to confusion and less accurate responses.

Types of Prompts

1. Open-ended Prompts: These prompts allow the AI to generate a wide range of responses. Example: "Tell me about the history of artificial intelligence."

2. Closed-ended Prompts: These prompts are more restrictive and guide the AI to a specific type of response. Example: "List the top five programming languages used in AI development."

3. Instruction-based Prompts: These prompts provide specific instructions for the AI to follow. Example: "Write a summary of the latest advancements in AI technology."

Crafting Effective Prompts

1. Define the Objective: Start by clearly defining what you want to achieve with the prompt. Are you looking for information, creative content, or a specific type of analysis?

2. Use Simple Language: Avoid jargon and complex sentences. Use simple, straightforward language to ensure the AI understands the prompt.

3. Incorporate Keywords: Use relevant keywords that are central to the topic. This helps the AI focus on the important aspects of the prompt.

4. Provide Examples: If possible, provide examples of the desired output. This can guide the AI in generating responses that meet

your expectations.

5. Iterate and Refine: Don't be afraid to iterate on your prompts. Test different versions and refine them based on the quality of the responses you receive.

Common Pitfalls and How to Avoid Them

1. Vagueness: Avoid vague prompts that lack direction. Example of a vague prompt: "Tell me something interesting." Instead, be specific: "Tell me an interesting fact about space exploration."
2. Overloading: Don't overload the prompt with too much information or multiple questions. Break it down into smaller, manageable parts.
3. Bias: Be mindful of any biases that might be present in your prompt. Ensure that your prompt is neutral and does not lead the AI to a biased response.

Advanced Techniques

1. Contextual Prompts: Use previous interactions or additional context to guide the AI. Example: "Based on our previous discussion about renewable energy, can you explain the benefits of solar power?"
2. Multi-turn Prompts: Engage the AI in a multi-turn conversation to build on previous responses. This can help in generating more detailed and nuanced outputs.
3. Role-playing Prompts: Assign a role to the AI to guide its responses. Example: "As a financial advisor, what would you recommend for a balanced investment portfolio?"

Practical Applications

1. Content Creation: Use prompts to generate articles, blog posts, or creative writing pieces. Example: "Write a 500-word article on the impact of AI on healthcare."
2. Data Analysis: Craft prompts to analyze data and generate insights. Example: "Analyze the sales data for the last quarter and identify any trends."
3. Customer Support: Develop prompts for automated customer support systems. Example: "Provide troubleshooting steps for a user experiencing connectivity issues with their router."

Conclusion

Crafting the perfect prompt is a skill that improves with practice. By understanding the key elements and techniques, you can create prompts that elicit high-quality responses from AI models. Remember to be clear, specific, and concise, and always provide enough context to guide the AI effectively.

Summary

- Clarity: Ensure your prompt is clear and unambiguous.
- Specificity: Be specific about what you want.
- Context: Provide enough background information.
- Conciseness: Keep it short and to the point.
- Iterate and Refine: Continuously improve your prompts based on feedback.

By following these guidelines, you can master the art of prompt crafting and unlock the full potential of AI models for your needs.

5

Applied AI Prompting

In this chapter, we will explore specific examples of effective AI prompts across various contexts. These examples will illustrate how to craft prompts that elicit high-quality responses from AI models, tailored to different needs and scenarios.

Example 1: Content Creation

- Context: Writing a blog post on the benefits of remote work.
- Prompt: "Write a 700-word blog post discussing the benefits of remote work. Include points on increased productivity, work-life balance, and cost savings for both employees and employers. Provide real-world examples and statistics to support each point."
- Why It Works: This prompt is clear, specific, and provides detailed instructions on what to include in the blog post. It also sets a word limit, which helps the AI understand the expected length of the response.

Example 2: Customer Support

- Context: Assisting a customer with troubleshooting a Wi-Fi connectivity issue.
- Prompt: "Provide step-by-step troubleshooting instructions for a customer experiencing Wi-Fi connectivity issues with their router. Include checks for physical connections, router settings, and potential interference sources. Offer solutions for common problems such as weak signal and no internet access."
- Why It Works: This prompt is specific and structured, guiding the AI to provide a comprehensive troubleshooting guide. It covers various aspects of the issue, ensuring that the response is thorough and helpful.

Example 3: Educational Assistance

- Context: Explaining a complex scientific concept to a high school student.
- Prompt: "Explain the concept of photosynthesis to a high school student. Use simple language and provide a step-by-step breakdown of the process. Include examples of how plants use sunlight to produce energy and the importance of photosynthesis in the ecosystem."
- Why It Works: This prompt is tailored to the audience (a high school student) and specifies the need for simple language and a step-by-step explanation. It also highlights key points to cover, ensuring the response is educational and accessible.

Example 4: Data Analysis

- Context: Analyzing sales data to identify trends.
- Prompt: "Analyze the sales data for the last quarter and identify any significant trends. Focus on changes in sales volume, revenue, and customer demographics. Provide visualizations such as charts or graphs to illustrate the trends and offer insights on potential causes."
- Why It Works: This prompt is detailed and specific, guiding the AI to focus on particular aspects of the sales data. It also requests visualizations, which can help in presenting the analysis more effectively.

Example 5: Creative Writing

- Context: Writing a short story with a specific theme.
- Prompt: "Write a 1,000-word short story set in a dystopian future where technology controls every aspect of human life. The protagonist should be a young rebel who discovers a way to break free from the technological control. Include elements of suspense and a surprising twist at the end."
- Why It Works: This prompt provides a clear setting, theme, and character for the story. It also specifies the desired length and key elements to include, which helps the AI generate a cohesive and engaging narrative.

Example 6: Technical Documentation

- Context: Creating a user manual for a new software application.
- Prompt: "Create a user manual for a new project management software application. Include sections on installation, basic usage, advanced features, and troubleshooting. Use clear and concise language, and provide screenshots to illustrate key steps."
- Why It Works: This prompt is structured and detailed, outlining the sections to include in the user manual. It also emphasizes the need for clear language and visual aids, which are essential for effective technical documentation.

These examples demonstrate how to craft effective AI prompts across different contexts. By being clear, specific, and providing detailed instructions, you can guide the AI to produce high-quality responses tailored to your needs. Whether you are creating content, providing customer support, or analyzing data, the principles of good prompt crafting remain the same.

Summary

- Content Creation: Provide detailed instructions and specify the desired length and key points.
- Customer Support: Structure the prompt to cover various aspects of the issue and offer comprehensive solutions.
- Educational Assistance: Tailor the prompt to the audience and use simple language.
- Data Analysis: Focus on specific aspects of the data and request visualizations.
- Creative Writing: Provide a clear setting, theme, and character, and specify key elements to include.
- Technical Documentation: Outline the sections to include and emphasize the need for clear language and visual aids.

By applying these principles, you can craft prompts that effectively harness the power of AI models for a wide range of applications.

6

Text and Image Models

Integrating Visual and Linguistic Elements

In the realm of artificial intelligence, the convergence of text and image models represents a significant leap forward. This chapter explores how prompt engineering extends beyond the written word, encompassing the realm of images and how they interact with text. Understanding this integration is crucial for prompt engineers who aim to leverage AI's full potential in creating rich, multimedia content.

The Emergence of Text-Image Models

Text-image models are AI systems that understand and generate content combining both textual and visual elements. These models, such as DALL-E and MidJourney, represent a fusion of natural language processing (NLP) and computer vision, enabling them to interpret and create images based on textual descriptions.

Understanding the Mechanics

At their core, text-image models are trained on vast datasets containing both images and their corresponding textual descriptions. This training enables them to recognize patterns and relationships between text and visual elements, allowing them to generate images that accurately reflect given text prompts.

Crafting Effective Text-Image Prompts

Creating prompts for text-image models requires a unique approach, blending linguistic clarity with visual imagination:

1. **Descriptive Precision**: The prompt should vividly describe the desired image, including details about objects, colors, settings, and mood.
2. **Contextual Relevance**: The text should provide context that guides the model in understanding the scene or concept being depicted.
3. **Balancing Creativity and Clarity**: While creativity is essential, overly abstract or ambiguous prompts can lead to unpredictable results.

Applications of Text-Image Models

Text-image models have a wide range of applications:

1. **Creative Arts**: Generating unique artworks, illustrations, and designs based on specific themes or styles.
2. **Marketing and Advertising**: Creating visually appealing content for campaigns, tailored to specific narratives or brand messages.
3. **Educational Content**: Producing illustrative material for educational purposes, making complex concepts easier to understand.

4. **Entertainment**: Developing concept art for movies, video games, and other forms of media.

Best Practices in Text-Image Prompt Engineering

To harness the power of text-image models effectively, consider the following best practices:

1. **Understand the Model's Capabilities**: Familiarize yourself with the specific text-image model you are using, including its strengths and limitations.
2. **Use Descriptive Language**: Employ vivid and descriptive language in your prompts to guide the model in visualizing the intended image.
3. **Iterative Refinement**: Be prepared to refine and adjust your prompts based on the outputs, as perfecting the text-image correlation often requires several attempts.
4. **Ethical Considerations**: Be mindful of ethical implications, especially when creating images involving people or sensitive subjects.

Challenges in Text-Image Prompt Engineering

Working with text-image models presents unique challenges:

1. **Interpreting Abstract Concepts**: Models may struggle with abstract or conceptual prompts, leading to varied interpretations.
2. **Managing Expectations**: The generated images may not always align perfectly with the envisioned concept, requiring adjustments and reiterations.
3. **Data Bias and Ethical Concerns**: Like text-based models, text-

image models can reflect biases present in their training data, necessitating careful prompt crafting.

The Role of Creativity and Innovation

Creativity is paramount in text-image prompt engineering. The ability to imagine and articulate a visual concept through text is a skill that blends artistic vision with technical understanding. This creative process opens up new avenues for innovation in various fields, from art and design to technology and media.

Advanced Techniques in Text-Image Prompt Engineering

As you gain experience, explore advanced techniques like:

1. **Layered Descriptions**: Building prompts with layered details, gradually adding elements to refine the image.
2. **Combining Multiple Concepts**: Merging different ideas or themes in a single prompt to create complex or surreal images.
3. **Interactive Refinement**: Using the model's outputs as a basis for further refinement, iteratively guiding the AI towards the desired result.

The Future of Text-Image Models

The field of text-image models is rapidly evolving, with ongoing advancements in AI capabilities. Future models are likely to offer even greater precision, creativity, and understanding of complex prompts. This evolution will further enhance the role of prompt engineering in creating visually rich and contextually meaningful content.

Conclusion

Text-image models represent a fascinating intersection of language and visual art, enabled by the power of AI. Crafting effective prompts for these models requires a unique blend of linguistic skill, artistic vision, and technical understanding. This chapter has laid the groundwork for harnessing the potential of text-image models, setting the stage for more detailed explorations in subsequent chapters.

7

Emerging Models in AI

Navigating the New Frontiers

The landscape of artificial intelligence (AI) is continuously evolving, with emerging models pushing the boundaries of what's possible. This chapter explores the latest advancements in AI, focusing on models that extend beyond traditional text and image processing. We'll delve into the realms of text-to-speech, text-audio, and speech-to-text models, examining their implications for prompt engineering.

Text-to-Speech (TTS) Models

Text-to-speech models convert written text into spoken words, mimicking human speech. These models have evolved significantly, offering more natural and expressive voice outputs.

1. **Understanding TTS Models**: TTS models use deep learning algorithms to generate speech that sounds increasingly human-like. They analyze text for tone, emotion, and context to produce appropriate vocal expressions.

2. **Prompt Engineering for TTS**: Crafting prompts for TTS involves more than just writing text; it requires an understanding of how text translates into speech. Considerations include tone, inflection, pacing, and emotional undertones.
3. **Applications**: TTS models are used in audiobooks, virtual assistants, accessibility tools for the visually impaired, and more.

Text-Audio Models

Text-audio models are an exciting area of AI, combining text processing with audio analysis and generation. These models can generate audio content based on textual descriptions or modify existing audio in response to text prompts.

1. **Mechanics of Text-Audio Models**: These models understand both the textual and auditory aspects of content, allowing them to create or alter audio based on text inputs.
2. **Prompt Engineering Challenges**: Crafting prompts for text-audio models requires a deep understanding of both text and sound. Prompts must be detailed and contextually rich to guide the model accurately.
3. **Applications**: From creating music based on descriptive prompts to generating sound effects for gaming and film, the applications are vast and varied.

Speech-to-Text (STT) Models

Speech-to-text models transcribe spoken words into written text. These models have become increasingly accurate, capable of understanding various accents, dialects, and even noisy environments.

1. **Understanding STT Models**: STT models use algorithms to process and transcribe speech, dealing with challenges like accents, speech impediments, and background noise.
2. **Prompt Engineering for STT**: While STT models primarily deal with input speech, prompt engineering can be involved in setting parameters for transcription, like language settings, recognition of specific terminologies, or handling of non-verbal cues.
3. **Applications**: STT models are crucial in real-time transcription services, voice command devices, and accessibility tools for hearing-impaired individuals.

Best Practices in Engineering Prompts for Emerging Models

1. **Understand the Model's Capabilities and Limitations**: Each model type has its strengths and weaknesses. Understanding these is key to crafting effective prompts.
2. **Contextual Richness**: Whether it's TTS, text-audio, or STT, providing rich context in prompts helps the model generate more accurate and relevant outputs.
3. **Iterative Testing and Refinement**: Working with emerging models often involves a process of trial and error. Regular testing and refinement of prompts are essential.
4. **Ethical Considerations**: As with all AI models, ethical considerations are paramount. This includes ensuring privacy in STT models and avoiding biases in TTS and text-audio models.

Challenges in Prompt Engineering for Emerging Models

1. **Complexity of Integration**: Emerging models often integrate multiple AI disciplines, making prompt engineering more complex.

2. **Data Quality and Availability**: The effectiveness of these models depends on the quality and diversity of the data they are trained on.
3. **Handling Ambiguity and Nuance**: Especially in speech-related models, handling nuances like sarcasm, humor, or regional dialects can be challenging.

The Role of Innovation in Prompt Engineering

Innovation is at the heart of prompt engineering for emerging models. As these models open new possibilities, prompt engineers must think creatively and experimentally to explore their full potential.

Advanced Techniques in Prompt Engineering for Emerging Models

1. **Multi-modal Prompts**: Combining text, audio, and even visual elements in prompts to guide models more effectively.
2. **Contextual Layering**: Building prompts with multiple layers of context, especially useful in text-audio models.
3. **Feedback Loops**: Using the output of models as feedback to refine and adjust prompts for better accuracy.

The Future of Emerging Models in AI

The future of AI is bright with the continuous development of emerging models. We can expect more sophisticated, integrated, and intuitive models, blurring the lines between human and machine capabilities.

Conclusion

Emerging models in AI represent the cutting edge of technology, offering new ways to interact with and utilize AI. Prompt engineering for these models requires a blend of technical knowledge, creativity, and ethical consideration. This chapter has provided an overview of these models and guidance on how to craft effective prompts for them, setting the stage for more detailed explorations in subsequent chapters.

8

Developing a Prompt Engineering Mindset

Cultivating the Right Approach

Prompt engineering is not just a technical skill; it's a mindset. This chapter explores the cognitive and philosophical aspects of prompt engineering, focusing on how to cultivate the right approach to maximize the potential of AI interactions. A prompt engineer must balance technical acumen with creativity, critical thinking, and ethical considerations.

Understanding the Prompt Engineering Mindset

A prompt engineering mindset involves a deep understanding of how AI models interpret and respond to language. It requires an appreciation for the nuances of communication, a keen sense of curiosity, and a willingness to experiment and learn from failures.

1. Curiosity and Continuous Learning

The field of AI is constantly evolving, and so must the prompt engineer.

A mindset of continuous learning and curiosity is essential. This involves staying updated with the latest advancements in AI, understanding new models and techniques, and being open to experimenting with new approaches.

2. Critical Thinking and Problem-Solving

Effective prompt engineering requires critical thinking. It's about understanding not just what to ask an AI model, but how to ask it. This involves analyzing the task at hand, anticipating how the AI might interpret different phrasings, and creatively solving problems that arise.

3. Creativity and Innovation

Creativity is at the heart of prompt engineering. It's about thinking outside the box and finding new ways to interact with AI. This could mean experimenting with different styles of prompts, using metaphors or analogies, or even 'thinking like the AI' to better understand how it processes information.

4. Ethical Awareness and Responsibility

Prompt engineers must be aware of the ethical implications of their work. This includes understanding the potential biases in AI models, the impact of prompts on AI behavior, and the broader societal implications of AI technology.

Best Practices for Developing a Prompt Engineering Mindset

1. **Embrace Experimentation**: Don't be afraid to try new things and learn from failures. Experimentation is key to understanding

what works and what doesn't.

2. **Seek Feedback and Collaborate**: Collaborate with others and seek feedback on your prompts. Different perspectives can provide valuable insights.

3. **Reflect on Successes and Failures**: Take time to reflect on what worked well and what didn't. Understanding your successes and failures is crucial for growth.

4. **Stay Informed and Educated**: Keep up with the latest developments in AI and prompt engineering. Attend workshops, read relevant literature, and engage with the community.

Challenges in Developing a Prompt Engineering Mindset

1. **Overcoming Biases**: We all have inherent biases, and these can influence how we craft prompts. Being aware of and actively working to overcome these biases is crucial.

2. **Adapting to Rapid Changes**: The AI field is rapidly evolving, and keeping up can be challenging. Adapting to new models and techniques requires flexibility and a willingness to learn.

3. **Balancing Technical and Creative Aspects**: Finding the right balance between technical precision and creative flair can be challenging but is essential for effective prompt engineering.

The Role of Ethics in Prompt Engineering

Ethics play a crucial role in prompt engineering. This includes:

1. **Ensuring Fairness and Avoiding Bias**: Striving to create prompts that are fair and unbiased, and that do not perpetuate harmful stereotypes or misinformation.

2. **Respecting Privacy and Confidentiality**: Being mindful of

privacy concerns, especially when dealing with sensitive data.

3. **Considering Societal Impact**: Understanding the broader impact of AI technology on society and striving to use it in a way that benefits humanity.

Advanced Techniques for Developing a Prompt Engineering Mindset

1. **Meta-Cognition**: Thinking about how you think. This involves reflecting on your thought processes and decision-making strategies when crafting prompts.
2. **Scenario Planning**: Imagining different scenarios and how the AI might respond to various prompts. This helps in anticipating potential issues and crafting more effective prompts.
3. **Cross-Disciplinary Learning**: Drawing insights from other fields such as psychology, linguistics, and philosophy to enrich your understanding of communication and AI.

The Future of the Prompt Engineering Mindset

As AI continues to advance, the prompt engineering mindset will become increasingly important. Future developments in AI will likely require even more sophisticated understanding and creativity in prompt crafting.

Conclusion

Developing a prompt engineering mindset is about more than just learning technical skills. It's about cultivating a way of thinking that balances curiosity, creativity, critical thinking, and ethical awareness. By embracing this mindset, prompt engineers can unlock the full potential of AI, creating more effective, innovative, and responsible AI interactions.

9

Best Practices in Prompt Engineering

Mastering the Craft of Prompt Crafting

Prompt engineering is an essential skill in the realm of AI, where the quality of input significantly influences the quality of output. This chapter delves into the best practices for crafting effective prompts, ensuring that interactions with AI are productive, efficient, and aligned with intended outcomes.

Understanding the Importance of Effective Prompts

Effective prompts are the cornerstone of successful AI interactions. They guide the AI to understand and respond in a way that meets the user's needs. The art of crafting these prompts involves a deep understanding of the AI's capabilities, the context of the task, and the desired outcome.

1. Clarity and Specificity

The most effective prompts are clear and specific. Vague or ambiguous prompts can lead to misinterpretation and unsatisfactory responses from the AI. It's crucial to be precise in what you're asking or instructing the AI to do.

2. Contextualization

Providing context in your prompts helps the AI understand the request within the correct framework. This is particularly important for complex tasks or when the AI needs background information to generate a relevant response.

3. Conciseness

While providing context is important, conciseness is equally crucial. Overly verbose prompts can confuse the AI or lead it down unnecessary tangents. The challenge lies in balancing detail with brevity.

4. Structuring Prompts Effectively

The structure of a prompt can significantly impact the AI's response. This includes the order in which information is presented, the use of keywords, and the framing of questions or commands.

5. Iterative Approach

Prompt engineering often involves an iterative process. Based on the AI's responses, prompts may need to be adjusted and refined. This process of trial and error is a normal part of finding the most effective way to communicate with the AI.

Best Practices for Crafting Prompts

1. **Understand Your AI**: Familiarize yourself with the specific AI model you're working with, including its strengths, limitations, and quirks.
2. **Use Natural Language**: Write prompts in natural, human-like language. This helps the AI process them more effectively.
3. **Test and Refine**: Don't be afraid to rephrase or adjust your prompts based on the AI's responses.
4. **Avoid Leading Questions**: Be neutral in your phrasing to avoid biasing the AI's responses.
5. **Use Examples**: When appropriate, include examples in your prompts to guide the AI's understanding.

Challenges in Prompt Engineering

1. **Dealing with Ambiguity**: AI can struggle with ambiguous language, leading to varied interpretations.
2. **Managing Complexity**: Complex tasks may require complex prompts, which can be challenging to craft effectively.
3. **Ethical Considerations**: Ensuring that prompts do not inadvertently lead to biased or unethical responses from the AI.

Ethical Considerations in Prompt Engineering

Ethics play a crucial role in prompt engineering. This includes being mindful of potential biases, respecting privacy, and considering the societal impact of AI responses.

Advanced Techniques in Prompt Engineering

1. **Chain of Thought Prompting**: Guiding the AI through a logical sequence of thoughts to arrive at a conclusion.

2. **Counterfactual Thinking**: Using 'what if' scenarios to explore different outcomes or perspectives.
3. **Prompt Templates**: Developing templates for common types of requests or tasks can streamline the prompt engineering process.

The Role of Feedback in Prompt Engineering

Feedback, both from the AI and from human users, is invaluable in refining prompts. It provides insights into how the AI interprets different phrasings and what types of prompts are most effective.

The Future of Prompt Engineering

As AI technology continues to evolve, the field of prompt engineering will also advance. Future developments may include more intuitive AI models that require less precise prompting, but the fundamental principles of clear, contextual, and concise communication will remain essential.

Conclusion

Mastering the art of prompt engineering is crucial for anyone looking to leverage the power of AI effectively. By adhering to best practices and continually refining their approach, prompt engineers can ensure that their interactions with AI are as productive and meaningful as possible.

10

Zero-Shot and Few-Shot Prompting

Exploring Advanced Prompting Techniques

In the evolving landscape of AI and prompt engineering, zero-shot and few-shot learning represent groundbreaking techniques. This chapter delves into these advanced prompting methods, exploring how they enable AI models to perform tasks with minimal to no prior examples.

Understanding Zero-Shot and Few-Shot Learning

Zero-shot learning refers to the AI's ability to understand and perform tasks it has never explicitly been trained to do. Few-shot learning, on the other hand, involves the AI learning from a very small number of examples. Both techniques are significant in the context of prompt engineering, as they reduce the need for extensive training data.

1. The Significance of Zero-Shot Learning

Zero-shot learning is particularly powerful because it allows AI models to generalize from their training and apply learned concepts to entirely new scenarios. This capability is crucial for prompt engineers, as it means AI can handle a wide variety of tasks without needing specific training for each.

2. The Role of Few-Shot Learning

Few-shot learning is essential when dealing with niche or specialized tasks for which large datasets may not exist. By understanding and adapting from a few examples, AI models can perform these tasks effectively, making them more versatile and adaptable.

Best Practices in Zero-Shot and Few-Shot Prompting

1. **Clear and Descriptive Prompts**: In zero-shot and few-shot learning, the clarity and descriptiveness of prompts are paramount. The AI relies heavily on the information provided in the prompt to understand and execute the task.
2. **Use of Analogies and Examples**: Using analogies or related examples in prompts can help guide the AI's understanding, especially in zero-shot scenarios.
3. **Iterative Refinement**: Given the minimal data, prompts may require more iterative testing and refinement to achieve the desired outcome.
4. **Balancing Specificity and Flexibility**: Prompts should be specific enough to guide the AI but also flexible enough to allow for generalization.

Challenges in Zero-Shot and Few-Shot Prompting

1. **Unpredictability of Responses**: With minimal training data, AI responses can be less predictable, requiring more careful crafting

and testing of prompts.

2. **Handling Ambiguity**: AI models may struggle with ambiguity in zero-shot and few-shot scenarios, making it crucial to craft clear and unambiguous prompts.

3. **Ethical and Bias Considerations**: With limited examples, there's a higher risk of biases influencing the AI's responses, necessitating careful consideration and testing.

Ethical Considerations in Advanced Prompting Techniques

Ethical considerations are particularly important in zero-shot and few-shot learning due to the increased reliance on the AI's inherent biases and generalizations.

Advanced Techniques in Zero-Shot and Few-Shot Prompting

1. **Prompt Engineering as Teaching**: Think of prompt engineering in these scenarios as teaching the AI, guiding its understanding and response generation.

2. **Contextual Layering**: Providing layered context in prompts can help the AI better understand and respond to complex tasks.

3. **Feedback Loops**: Using the AI's responses as feedback to refine and adjust prompts for better accuracy and relevance.

The Role of Creativity in Zero-Shot and Few-Shot Prompting

Creativity plays a crucial role in these advanced prompting techniques. Prompt engineers must think outside the box to effectively guide AI models that have limited training in specific tasks.

The Future of Zero-Shot and Few-Shot Learning in AI

As AI technology continues to evolve, zero-shot and few-shot learning will become increasingly sophisticated, enabling AI models to handle a broader range of tasks with less specific training.

Conclusion

Zero-shot and few-shot learning represent exciting frontiers in AI and prompt engineering. By mastering these advanced prompting techniques, prompt engineers can unlock new levels of AI versatility and adaptability, enabling AI models to tackle a wide range of tasks with minimal prior training.

11

Chain of Thought Prompting

Harnessing Logical Sequences in AI Responses

Chain of thought prompting represents a significant advancement in the field of prompt engineering. This chapter delves into this technique, which involves guiding AI through a series of logical steps to arrive at a conclusion. It's a powerful tool for eliciting more detailed, reasoned responses from AI models.

Understanding Chain of Thought Prompting

Chain of thought prompting is based on the principle of leading AI through a step-by-step reasoning process. Instead of expecting the AI to jump directly to an answer, the prompt is structured to encourage the AI to 'think out loud,' showing its reasoning at each step.

1. The Importance of Logical Sequencing

The key to successful chain of thought prompting is the logical sequence of the steps. Each step in the reasoning process must logically follow from the previous one, guiding the AI towards the final answer or conclusion.

2. Enhancing AI Comprehension and Response Quality

This approach not only improves the quality of the AI's responses but also enhances its comprehension of complex tasks. By breaking down a task into smaller, logical steps, the AI can handle more complex reasoning that might be challenging with direct prompting.

Best Practices in Chain of Thought Prompting

1. **Structured and Sequential Prompts**: Craft prompts that are structured in a clear, step-by-step manner, guiding the AI through the reasoning process.
2. **Encouraging Detailed Responses**: Frame prompts in a way that encourages the AI to provide detailed, step-by-step explanations, rather than concise answers.
3. **Testing and Refinement**: Chain of thought prompts often require testing and refinement to perfect the logical flow and ensure accurate conclusions.
4. **Balancing Guidance and Flexibility**: While it's important to guide the AI's thought process, allowing some flexibility for the AI to apply its reasoning capabilities is also crucial.

Challenges in Chain of Thought Prompting

1. **Complexity of Crafting Prompts**: Creating effective chain of thought prompts can be complex, requiring a deep understanding of the task and the logical steps involved.
2. **Predicting AI Behavior**: Anticipating how an AI model will interpret and follow through a chain of thought can be challenging.
3. **Maintaining Logical Consistency**: Ensuring that each step in

the chain of thought is logically consistent and leads appropriately to the next can be demanding.

Ethical Considerations in Chain of Thought Prompting

Ethical considerations in chain of thought prompting include ensuring that the reasoning process does not perpetuate biases or lead to unethical conclusions.

Advanced Techniques in Chain of Thought Prompting

1. **Nested Reasoning**: Incorporating nested layers of reasoning within prompts, where one chain of thought leads to another.
2. **Hypothetical Scenarios**: Using hypothetical scenarios within prompts to explore complex reasoning or problem-solving.
3. **Counterfactual Reasoning**: Encouraging the AI to consider alternative outcomes or scenarios as part of its reasoning process.

The Role of Creativity in Chain of Thought Prompting

Creativity is essential in crafting chain of thought prompts. It involves imagining how an AI might break down a problem and creatively structuring prompts to guide this process.

The Future of Chain of Thought in AI

As AI models become more sophisticated, their ability to handle complex chain of thought prompts will improve. This advancement will enable more nuanced and detailed AI interactions, particularly in fields requiring complex decision-making and problem-solving.

Conclusion

Chain of thought prompting is a powerful technique in prompt engineering, enabling AI to handle complex reasoning tasks more effectively. By mastering this approach, prompt engineers can significantly enhance the capabilities of AI models, leading to more insightful, detailed, and useful AI responses.

12

AI Hallucinations and Error Handling

Navigating the Challenges of AI Misinterpretations

AI hallucinations, a term used to describe instances where AI models generate incorrect or nonsensical information, present a significant challenge in prompt engineering. This chapter explores strategies for identifying, understanding, and mitigating these errors, ensuring more reliable and accurate AI interactions.

Understanding AI Hallucinations

AI hallucinations occur when an AI model generates responses that are factually incorrect, irrelevant, or nonsensical. These errors can arise from limitations in the AI's training data, misinterpretation of prompts, or inherent biases in the model.

1. Identifying AI Hallucinations

Recognizing AI hallucinations involves understanding the difference between a plausible but incorrect response and one that is clearly a result of the AI's misinterpretation or fabrication. Key indicators include responses that are factually inaccurate, logically inconsistent, or irrelevant to the prompt.

2. Causes of AI Hallucinations

AI hallucinations can be caused by various factors, including:

- **Insufficient or Biased Training Data**: If the AI's training data is limited or biased, it may generate responses based on these limitations or biases.
- **Complex or Ambiguous Prompts**: Prompts that are too complex or ambiguous can lead the AI to 'guess' or fabricate responses.
- **Model Limitations**: Inherent limitations in the AI model's understanding of context or specific subjects can also lead to hallucinations.

Best Practices for Handling AI Hallucinations

1. **Clear and Specific Prompts**: Crafting clear and specific prompts can reduce the likelihood of AI hallucinations by providing the AI with a clear understanding of the task.
2. **Regular Testing and Validation**: Regularly testing the AI's responses and validating them against reliable sources can help identify and correct hallucinations.
3. **Feedback Mechanisms**: Implementing feedback mechanisms where users can report hallucinations can help improve the AI's accuracy over time.
4. **Understanding Model Limitations**: Being aware of the specific limitations of the AI model being used can help in crafting prompts that avoid known areas of weakness.

Strategies for Error Correction and Mitigation

1. **Prompt Refinement**: Refining prompts to be more direct and specific can help reduce the likelihood of hallucinations.
2. **Contextual Clues**: Providing additional context in prompts can guide the AI to more accurate responses.
3. **Fallback Mechanisms**: Implementing fallback mechanisms, such as default responses or redirections to human operators, can mitigate the impact of hallucinations.

Ethical Considerations in Handling AI Hallucinations

Handling AI hallucinations ethically involves ensuring that responses do not propagate misinformation, stereotypes, or harmful content. Prompt engineers must be vigilant in monitoring and correcting such errors.

Advanced Techniques in Handling AI Hallucinations

1. **Chain of Thought Verification**: Using chain of thought prompting to encourage the AI to explain its reasoning, making it easier to spot and correct hallucinations.
2. **Cross-Referencing Responses**: Cross-referencing the AI's responses with trusted data sources or other AI models for verification.
3. **Custom Error Handling Protocols**: Developing custom protocols for handling different types of hallucinations, tailored to the specific use case and AI model.

The Role of Transparency in AI Interactions

Transparency is crucial in AI interactions, especially when dealing with hallucinations. Users should be made aware of the potential for errors and the steps taken to mitigate them.

The Future of AI Hallucinations and Error Handling

As AI technology advances, models will become more sophisticated in understanding context and reducing the occurrence of hallucinations. However, prompt engineers will continue to play a crucial role in guiding AI models to accurate and reliable responses.

Conclusion

AI hallucinations and error handling are critical aspects of prompt engineering, requiring a combination of technical skill, vigilance, and ethical consideration. By understanding and implementing strategies to mitigate these issues, prompt engineers can enhance the reliability and trustworthiness of AI interactions.

13

Vectors and Text Embeddings in AI

Delving into the Technical Backbone of AI Language Processing

Vectors and text embeddings represent the foundational technology enabling AI's understanding and processing of language. This chapter explores these concepts, crucial for prompt engineers to understand how AI interprets and responds to prompts.

Understanding Vectors and Text Embeddings

In AI, particularly in natural language processing (NLP), vectors and text embeddings are methods used to represent words and phrases in a numerical format that AI models can understand and process. They are the bridge between the human language and the AI's computational capabilities.

1. The Role of Vectors in AI

Vectors are essentially lists of numbers that represent various features of a word or phrase. In AI, these vectors help in quantifying and analyzing textual data. Each dimension of a vector can represent a different feature or aspect of the word, such as its meaning, context, or usage.

2. Text Embeddings Explained

Text embeddings are a more advanced form of vectors. They are high-dimensional spaces where words with similar meanings are positioned closer together. This positioning allows AI models to understand the relationships and nuances between different words and phrases.

Best Practices in Utilizing Vectors and Text Embeddings

1. **Understanding the Model's Language Capabilities**: Different AI models use different types of embeddings. Understanding the specific embeddings used by your AI model is crucial for effective prompt engineering.
2. **Contextual Relevance**: Since embeddings capture the context of words, ensuring that your prompts are contextually relevant is key to eliciting accurate responses.
3. **Balancing Brevity and Detail**: While detailed prompts can provide more context, they can also introduce noise. Balancing brevity and detail is essential for effective use of embeddings.

Challenges in Working with Vectors and Text Embeddings

1. **Complexity of Interpretation**: Understanding how an AI model interprets vectors and embeddings can be challenging, requiring a deep understanding of NLP.
2. **Handling Ambiguity**: Words with multiple meanings can have complex embeddings, making it challenging to craft prompts that guide the AI to the intended meaning.

3. **Model Limitations**: The AI's understanding is limited to what its embeddings can capture. Understanding these limitations is crucial for effective prompt engineering.

Ethical Considerations in Using Vectors and Text Embeddings

Ethical considerations include being aware of biases embedded in the AI's language model and ensuring that prompts do not inadvertently reinforce these biases.

Advanced Techniques in Utilizing Vectors and Text Embeddings

1. **Semantic Analysis**: Using an understanding of embeddings to craft prompts that align closely with the semantic context the AI is likely to interpret.
2. **Custom Embeddings**: For specialized applications, creating custom embeddings can improve the AI's performance on specific tasks.
3. **Embedding Visualization**: Visualizing text embeddings can provide insights into how the AI model understands and relates different concepts.

The Role of Experimentation in Understanding Embeddings

Experimentation is key in understanding how different prompts influence the AI's interpretation based on its embeddings. Testing various phrasings and structures can provide valuable insights.

The Future of Vectors and Text Embeddings in AI

As AI technology advances, we can expect more sophisticated embeddings that capture linguistic nuances more accurately. This advancement will enhance the AI's language processing capabilities, making prompt engineering more effective and intuitive.

Conclusion

Vectors and text embeddings are at the heart of AI's language processing capabilities. Understanding these concepts is crucial for prompt engineers to craft effective prompts that align with the AI's interpretation mechanisms. By mastering the use of vectors and text embeddings, prompt engineers can significantly enhance the AI's ability to understand and respond to human language.

14

Maintaining and Updating Prompt Libraries

Ensuring Relevance and Effectiveness Over Time

In the dynamic field of AI and prompt engineering, maintaining and updating prompt libraries is crucial for sustained effectiveness. This chapter focuses on strategies for keeping prompt libraries relevant, accurate, and aligned with evolving AI capabilities and user needs.

Understanding the Importance of Prompt Libraries

Prompt libraries are collections of prompts that have been tested and refined for specific tasks or interactions with AI models. They serve as valuable resources for efficiently handling recurring tasks or queries.

1. The Role of Prompt Libraries

Prompt libraries play a critical role in streamlining AI interactions. They provide a repository of effective prompts that can be reused or adapted, saving time and ensuring consistency in AI responses.

2. The Need for Regular Updates

As AI models evolve and user needs change, prompt libraries must be updated to maintain their relevance and effectiveness. This involves adding new prompts, refining existing ones, and removing outdated or ineffective prompts.

Best Practices in Maintaining Prompt Libraries

1. **Regular Review and Assessment**: Periodically review the prompt library to assess the effectiveness of each prompt and identify areas for improvement.
2. **User Feedback Integration**: Incorporate user feedback to understand how well prompts are performing and where adjustments are needed.
3. **Alignment with AI Model Updates**: Stay informed about updates to AI models and adjust prompts accordingly to leverage new capabilities or address changes.
4. **Categorization and Organization**: Organize the prompt library in a way that makes it easy to find and select the most appropriate prompts for different tasks.

Challenges in Maintaining Prompt Libraries

1. **Keeping Pace with AI Evolution**: AI models are continually evolving, and keeping prompt libraries aligned with these changes can be challenging.
2. **Managing a Growing Library**: As the library grows, ensuring that it remains organized and manageable can become increasingly difficult.
3. **Ensuring Quality and Relevance**: Continuously ensuring that

all prompts in the library are of high quality and relevant to current needs requires ongoing effort.

Strategies for Effective Prompt Library Updates

1. **Automated Monitoring Tools**: Implement tools to automatically monitor the performance of prompts and flag those that need review.
2. **Collaborative Maintenance**: Encourage collaboration among team members or users for maintaining and updating the prompt library.
3. **Version Control**: Use version control systems to track changes in prompts, allowing for easy rollback if updates lead to decreased effectiveness.

Ethical Considerations in Prompt Library Maintenance

Ethical considerations include ensuring that prompts do not perpetuate biases or misinformation and respecting user privacy and data security in the collection and use of feedback.

Advanced Techniques in Prompt Library Management

1. **Data-Driven Updates**: Use data analytics to understand prompt performance and guide updates.
2. **A/B Testing**: Regularly conduct A/B testing to compare the effectiveness of different prompts and refine the library based on results.
3. **Predictive Maintenance**: Implement predictive models to anticipate which prompts may become less effective over time and proactively update them.

The Role of Community in Prompt Library Development

Engaging with a broader community of prompt engineers and users can provide valuable insights and contributions to the prompt library, enhancing its diversity and effectiveness.

The Future of Prompt Libraries

As AI continues to advance, the role of prompt libraries will become increasingly important. Future developments may include more sophisticated tools for prompt management and the integration of AI-assisted prompt creation and refinement.

Conclusion

Maintaining and updating prompt libraries is a critical aspect of prompt engineering, ensuring that interactions with AI remain effective and relevant over time. By adopting best practices and leveraging advanced techniques, prompt engineers can create dynamic, responsive libraries that enhance the efficiency and quality of AI interactions.

15

Reporting and Analytics in Prompt Engineering

Measuring Success and Informing Strategies

In the field of prompt engineering, the ability to measure the effectiveness of prompts and understand user interactions through reporting and analytics is crucial. This chapter explores the methodologies and tools used to analyze prompt performance, providing insights for continuous improvement.

Understanding the Role of Reporting and Analytics

Reporting and analytics in prompt engineering involve collecting, analyzing, and interpreting data related to AI interactions. This process helps in understanding how well prompts are performing and guides decisions for refining them.

1. The Importance of Data-Driven Insights

Data-driven insights allow prompt engineers to objectively assess the effectiveness of their prompts. By analyzing user interactions and AI responses, engineers can identify patterns, successes, and areas for improvement.

2. Key Metrics in Prompt Engineering

Several metrics are crucial in evaluating prompt performance, including response accuracy, user satisfaction, engagement rates, and error rates. Understanding these metrics is essential for effective analysis.

Best Practices in Reporting and Analytics

1. **Comprehensive Data Collection**: Collect a wide range of data, including AI responses, user feedback, and interaction logs, to gain a holistic view of prompt performance.
2. **Regular Analysis**: Conduct regular analyses to track performance over time and identify trends or changes in AI interactions.
3. **User-Centric Approach**: Focus on metrics that reflect user satisfaction and engagement to ensure that prompts are meeting user needs.
4. **Iterative Improvement**: Use insights from analytics to continuously refine prompts, adopting an iterative approach to improvement.

Challenges in Prompt Engineering Analytics

1. **Interpreting Data Correctly**: Ensuring accurate interpretation of data can be challenging, especially when dealing with ambiguous or subjective metrics.
2. **Balancing Quantitative and Qualitative Insights**: Combining quantitative data with qualitative feedback is crucial for a well-

rounded understanding of prompt performance.

3. **Data Privacy and Security**: Managing data collection and analysis while respecting user privacy and adhering to data security regulations.

Strategies for Effective Analytics in Prompt Engineering

1. **Visualization Tools**: Utilize data visualization tools to make complex data more understandable and actionable.
2. **Segmentation and Comparative Analysis**: Segment data to compare different user groups, prompts, or time periods.
3. **Feedback Loops**: Implement feedback loops that allow users to provide direct input on AI interactions, enriching the data for analysis.

Ethical Considerations in Analytics

Ethical considerations include ensuring transparency in data collection and use, respecting user privacy, and avoiding biases in data interpretation and decision-making.

Advanced Techniques in Prompt Engineering Analytics

1. **Predictive Analytics**: Use predictive models to forecast future trends in prompt performance and user interactions.
2. **Natural Language Processing (NLP) for Feedback Analysis**: Employ NLP techniques to analyze qualitative feedback and extract meaningful insights.
3. **A/B Testing and Experimental Design**: Conduct A/B testing and controlled experiments to evaluate the effectiveness of different prompts.

The Role of Continuous Learning in Analytics

Continuous learning is key in prompt engineering analytics. Staying informed about the latest analytical tools and methodologies can significantly enhance the ability to derive meaningful insights from data.

The Future of Reporting and Analytics in AI

As AI technology advances, we can expect more sophisticated analytical tools and methodologies to emerge. These advancements will enable deeper insights and more effective prompt optimization.

Conclusion

Reporting and analytics play a critical role in prompt engineering, providing the insights needed to measure success and inform strategies for improvement. By adopting best practices and leveraging advanced analytical techniques, prompt engineers can ensure their prompts remain effective and relevant in the ever-evolving landscape of AI interactions.

16

Case Studies and Real-World Applications

Translating Theory into Practice

In prompt engineering, real-world applications and case studies provide invaluable insights into the practical aspects of the field. This chapter presents a series of case studies that illustrate the diverse applications of prompt engineering and the strategies employed to address various challenges.

Understanding the Value of Case Studies

Case studies in prompt engineering offer concrete examples of how theoretical concepts are applied in real-world scenarios. They provide a window into the challenges, strategies, and outcomes of prompt engineering in different contexts.

1. Diverse Applications

Prompt engineering finds applications across various domains, including customer service, content creation, education, healthcare, and more.

Each application presents unique challenges and opportunities for prompt engineering.

2. Learning from Successes and Failures

Analyzing both successful and unsuccessful cases helps in understanding what works and what doesn't in prompt engineering. These lessons are invaluable for refining strategies and approaches.

Case Study 1: Customer Service Chatbot

This case study explores the development of a customer service chatbot for a retail company. It highlights the challenges in crafting prompts that accurately interpret customer queries and provide helpful responses.

- **Challenge**: Handling a wide range of customer queries with varying levels of complexity.
- **Strategy**: Developing a comprehensive prompt library, categorizing prompts based on query types, and implementing an iterative refinement process.
- **Outcome**: Improved customer satisfaction and reduced response time.

Case Study 2: Educational AI Tutor

This case involves an AI tutor designed to assist students in learning a foreign language. The focus is on crafting prompts that facilitate language learning and comprehension.

- **Challenge**: Adapting prompts to different proficiency levels and learning styles.

- **Strategy**: Using data-driven insights to customize prompts and employing NLP techniques for language assessment.
- **Outcome**: Enhanced learning experiences and positive feedback from learners.

Case Study 3: Healthcare Diagnostic Tool

This case study examines the use of AI in diagnosing medical conditions based on patient symptoms and history.

- **Challenge**: Ensuring accuracy and sensitivity in handling medical information.
- **Strategy**: Collaborating with medical professionals to develop prompts, implementing strict privacy protocols, and continuous testing for accuracy.
- **Outcome**: A reliable diagnostic tool that supplements healthcare professionals.

Case Study 4: Content Creation for Marketing

Here, the focus is on using AI for generating creative content for marketing campaigns.

- **Challenge**: Producing original, engaging, and brand-aligned content.
- **Strategy**: Crafting prompts that encapsulate brand voice and style, and using A/B testing to gauge content effectiveness.
- **Outcome**: Diverse and innovative marketing content that resonates with the target audience.

Best Practices Derived from Case Studies

1. **Collaboration with Subject Matter Experts**: Collaborating with experts in the relevant field can greatly enhance the effectiveness of prompts.
2. **User-Centric Design**: Focusing on the end-user's needs and preferences in prompt design.
3. **Continuous Monitoring and Adaptation**: Regularly monitoring AI interactions and adapting prompts based on feedback and performance data.

Challenges Highlighted in Case Studies

1. **Balancing AI Capabilities and User Expectations**: Finding the right balance between what AI can realistically achieve and user expectations.
2. **Handling Sensitive Information**: Ensuring privacy and ethical handling of sensitive data, especially in fields like healthcare.
3. **Cultural and Contextual Relevance**: Crafting prompts that are culturally and contextually appropriate for the target audience.

Ethical Considerations in Real-World Applications

Ethical considerations are paramount, especially in applications involving sensitive data or significant impact on users' lives. Ensuring fairness, privacy, and transparency is crucial.

The Role of Innovation in Prompt Engineering Applications

Innovation is key to addressing the unique challenges presented in different applications. Creative problem-solving and novel approaches often lead to more effective and efficient AI interactions.

The Future of Prompt Engineering in Real-World Applications

As AI technology continues to evolve, the scope of prompt engineering in real-world applications will expand, offering new opportunities and challenges. Staying adaptable and innovative is essential for success in this dynamic field.

Case studies and real-world applications provide valuable lessons and insights into the practical aspects of prompt engineering. By analyzing these examples, prompt engineers can gain a deeper understanding of how to apply theoretical knowledge in diverse contexts, leading to more effective and impactful AI interactions.

17

The Future of Prompt Engineering

Anticipating Trends and Preparing for Advancements

As we stand at the forefront of technological innovation, the future of prompt engineering is poised for significant advancements. This chapter explores potential trends, emerging technologies, and the evolving landscape of AI, providing insights into how prompt engineering might adapt and thrive in the coming years.

Understanding the Evolution of AI and Its Impact

The future of prompt engineering is intrinsically linked to the evolution of AI. As AI models become more sophisticated, the role and techniques of prompt engineering will also evolve.

1. Advancements in AI Models

Future AI models are expected to be more intuitive, context-aware, and capable of handling complex and nuanced tasks. This will require prompt engineers to develop more sophisticated prompting strategies.

2. Increased Integration of AI in Daily Life

As AI becomes more integrated into various aspects of daily life, the demand for effective prompt engineering will grow. This integration will span diverse fields, from healthcare and education to entertainment and personal assistance.

Emerging Trends in Prompt Engineering

1. **Personalization and User-Centric Design**: Future prompt engineering will likely focus more on personalization, tailoring prompts to individual user preferences and histories.
2. **Ethical AI and Responsible Prompting**: As awareness of AI ethics grows, there will be a greater emphasis on crafting prompts that are fair, unbiased, and respectful of privacy and security.
3. **Cross-Disciplinary Approaches**: The intersection of AI with other fields like psychology, linguistics, and neuroscience will enrich prompt engineering practices.

Challenges and Opportunities

1. **Adapting to Rapid Technological Changes**: Keeping pace with rapid advancements in AI technology will be a continuous challenge for prompt engineers.
2. **Balancing Automation and Human Oversight**: Finding the right balance between automated prompting and human oversight will be crucial in maintaining the effectiveness and ethical integrity of AI interactions.
3. **Globalization and Cultural Sensitivity**: As AI reaches a global audience, prompt engineering will need to address linguistic diversity and cultural sensitivity.

Innovations on the Horizon

1. **AI-Assisted Prompt Engineering**: The use of AI to assist in crafting and refining prompts is an emerging area that could significantly enhance efficiency and effectiveness.
2. **Advanced Natural Language Understanding (NLU)**: Improvements in NLU will enable AI to comprehend and respond to prompts with greater depth and nuance.
3. **Interactive and Adaptive AI Systems**: Future AI systems are likely to be more interactive and adaptive, capable of learning from user interactions to improve over time.

Preparing for the Future

1. **Continuous Learning and Adaptation**: Staying informed about the latest developments in AI and prompt engineering will be essential for success in this field.
2. **Collaboration and Community Engagement**: Engaging with the prompt engineering community and collaborating across disciplines will foster innovation and shared learning.
3. **Ethical Considerations and Guidelines**: Developing and adhering to ethical guidelines will be crucial in guiding the responsible development of prompt engineering practices.

The Role of Education and Training

As the field evolves, education and training in prompt engineering will become more important. This includes formal education programs, online courses, workshops, and self-guided learning resources.

The Future of Work in Prompt Engineering

The demand for skilled prompt engineers is likely to grow, creating new career opportunities. This will include roles in developing, refining, and managing AI interactions across various industries.

The future of prompt engineering is bright and full of potential. As AI continues to advance, prompt engineers will play a crucial role in shaping how we interact with and benefit from this transformative technology. By staying adaptable, informed, and ethically grounded, prompt engineers can lead the way in harnessing the power of AI to improve lives and solve complex problems.